"For years I have been loo[...] tian high school grads: re[...] Christ-centered, and practical. Finally, I've found just the ticket— *Make College Count* is that book."

Chap Clark, author of *Hurt: Inside the World of Today's Teenagers*; professor of youth, family, and culture, Fuller Theological Seminary

"Christian college students hear a lot about what to *avoid* during their college years. So it's refreshing to encounter a book that explains what students should *embrace* in college. It's clear that Derek Melleby understands the world of today's students. His book proves the point as he rolls out wise and practical advice that will equip young people to make the most of their college experience and graduate as mature, effective followers of Jesus Christ."

Joseph M. Stowell, president of Cornerstone University

"*Make College Count* is just right! What Derek Melleby has done is find a way to come alongside someone on the way to college and offer guidance about things that matter most. His own rich vision of learning and life threads its way throughout, giving windows into the challenge and complexity of the college years with a playful seriousness that feels like that of a friend who honestly cares how it all turns out."

Steven Garber, director of The Washington Institute for Faith, Vocation & Culture; author of *The Fabric of Faithfulness*

"Perhaps there's not a more significant watershed event in a young person's life than high school graduation and the transition to college. But research and experience point to the fact many transitioning students either forget to or consciously decide not to pack up their faith with the rest of the stuff they are taking to college. The university years are the perfect time for students to grow *in* their faith. But by the time they have a diploma in hand, many have allowed the distractions of life and the idols of our culture to grow them *away* from their faith. *Make College Count* offers an accurate preview of college life. It encourages and equips students to thoughtfully make the most of college (and the rest of their lives) by embracing a real and vibrant faith that's not an extracurricular add-on but a foundation for *all* of life. This could be the most important book students read during their college years."

Walt Mueller, president of Center for
Parent/Youth Understanding

"With this great little book Derek Melleby offers a kind of Cliffs-Notes study guide for these critical years. His knowledge of college students allows him to write convincingly about both the adventures and the perils of college life. With good humor, savvy realism, sound biblical counsel, and practical advice, this book offers valuable insights for those who find themselves facing the big questions and the hard tests for the real-world curriculum of college life. And it's a short enough book that college students are likely to actually read it!"

Duffy Robbins, professor of youth ministry, Eastern University

"I am always leery when I pick up a book designed to be a gift book for high school graduates. They are mostly cheesy or condescending. Derek has written to college freshmen from a perspective that is wise yet hip, profound yet common sense, and complete yet not overwhelming. What a world we would have with an emerging generation of leaders who carefully consider the implications of being a follower of Christ. Both of my college-aged children will get a copy of *Make College Count*."

Allen Jackson, professor of youth and collegiate ministry,
New Orleans Baptist Theological Seminary

MAKE COLLEGE COUNT

A Faithful Guide to Life and Learning

Derek Melleby

BakerBooks

a division of Baker Publishing Group
Grand Rapids, Michigan

Published by Baker Books
a division of Baker Publishing Group
PO Box 6287, Grand Rapids, MI 49516-6287
www.bakerbooks.com

Paperback edition published 2018
ISBN 978-0-8010-9420-0

Printed in the United States of America

The Library of Congress has cataloged the hardcover edition as follows:
Melleby, Derek, 1977–
    Make college count : a faithful guide to life and learning / Derek
    Melleby.
        p.   cm.
    Includes bibliographical references (p.   ).
    ISBN 978-0-8010-1397-3 (pbk.)
    1. Christian college students—Religious life. I. Title.
BV4531.3.M355 2011
248.8'34—dc22   2010036358

In keeping with biblical principles of creation stewardship, Baker Publishing Group advocates the responsible use of our natural resources. As a member of the Green Press Initiative, our company uses recycled paper when possible. The text paper of this book is composed in part of post-consumer waste.

green press INITIATIVE

For my sons

Jacob Henry, Nathan John, and Simon Van

Contents

Contents

Foreword

I am a huge fan of young leaders. Much of my time is spent studying, writing on, and speaking about the spirituality, college lives, and career pursuits of sixteen- to twenty-nine-year-olds. I think this book is a fantastic resource for young people. Let me explain why.

For one thing, it will help you sort through an important transition—from high school to college. Everyone has choices. But as a college applicant and university student you'll have more options than most. Not only do you get to choose where to attend and what to study, but these alternatives and hundreds of other decisions literally affect the rest of your lives. In *Make College Count*, my friend Derek Melleby will help you see that the most important choices you have to make are not merely where to attend or what major to select. He shows how the bigger questions—who you are, why you are going to college, and what kind of person you want to become—are the most important. And they are the hardest to answer.

Second, I like this book because it assumes young people are intelligent, gifted, and *want* to grow. Derek asks big questions, but he does not give you easy answers, even though the book is easy to read. He believes you will wrestle with the questions he is raising. If you are holding this book, you are probably a young leader called by God to be faithful in whatever school, class, relationship, or career you choose. Take that seriously!

Finally, I recommend this book because I know Derek Melleby personally. I admire Derek's commitment to young people. He is a committed Christ follower who devotes tons of effort to help students make great decisions—about the big things and the small things. It all matters to Derek, because it all matters to God.

I wish I'd had this book during my college years. Having the right perspective about college changes everything. It would have helped me in dozens of ways.

Make College Count can help you make the most of your college years by preparing you in ways that go far beyond test preparation and social life. No pressure, right? After all, you are making choices that affect the rest of your life.

David Kinnaman
author of *unChristian* and *You Lost Me*
president of Barna Group

Getting Started

You deserve a round of applause. The people around you ought to be clapping and hoisting you up on their shoulders. After all, you're reading a graduation gift book. I graduated years ago and still haven't even opened the book I received on graduation day. So, how did you get yours? Was it from a well-intentioned relative—you know, the one who means well but just won't give in to the much more appreciated gift card? Or was it from your youth leader or pastor? Now, I don't know your youth leader, but I do know this: a wise gift decision was made! There are a lot of gift books out there, but this one is the best. Just ask my mom. If you knew my mom, you would know that she is not the kind of woman who would lead you astray. Trust me. She's an avid reader and has nothing to gain by telling other people how great this book is. She means it.

Perhaps you picked up this book because you are already in college and really want to make this time in your life count. Maybe you are early in your college experience or are looking for a fresh start. This book will be helpful to you too.

Why did I write this book? Good question. A few summers ago I was roasting a marshmallow at a family picnic. Seated next to me was my wife's younger cousin, David. David was about to head off to college, and at one point in our conversation he said, "All the advice I was given at graduation only told me what *not* to do: *don't get drunk, don't have sex*! I need to know what *to* do." I took a bite of my s'more and thought, *He's right.* The message most college-bound students hear is negative. It goes something like this: College is a dangerous place. Students spend their time binge drinking, doing drugs, and hooking up, and many Christians lose their faith. Christian students need to keep and defend their faith if they are going to be able to survive the attacks from professors and peers. The picture is grim.

There is some truth to this scenario, to be sure. College campuses can be dangerous places. There will be pressure to engage in social and intellectual activity that could be detrimental to your health and faith. No question. But if there is one message that I hope gets through in this book, it is this: *Christian students should not fear college.* The Christian faith offers a foundation and framework for you to make your time in college the best four (or five or even six!) years of your life. The Christian life is defined more by what we *do* rather than what we *don't do.* My prayer is that this book equips you with a vision to make the most of your college experience by growing in your faith, developing lasting friendships, and thinking more deeply about your place in God's world. But please don't take this book as another lecture trying to tell you what to do. Rather, consider it an invitation to envision college differently, to ask good questions before going to college, and to be pointed in the direction of helpful resources.

One more thing before we get started. The following chapters pose the seven most important questions that all college students need to ask before and during college. I've learned that if you don't take time to ask and wrestle with these questions now, you run the risk of others answering them for you when you get to campus. Cultivating an inquisitive mind is one of the most important skills you can learn in life. Learning to ask good questions and not settle for easy answers are habits and disciplines that need to be developed. I hope that this book helps you to think critically about college, about what is going on there, and about what is happening to you while you're there. What you learn by asking these big questions will be more valuable to you than any particular detail that you'll learn in the classroom once you arrive on campus.

As you are probably aware (and frustrated with to some degree!), much of your thinking has been done for you by others up until this point in life. Parents, pastors,

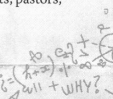

coaches, and teachers, out of concern for your well-being, have poured their lives into you, providing just about all of the opinions and advice that you can handle. Now, I have nothing against guidance. Had my mom not taught me how to do laundry, I probably wouldn't have had many friends in college. We all need to give more credit and thanks to those who have invested in our lives, even when we're convinced that we could do things on our own. While this book is a guide of sorts, I don't want it to be taken simply as advice. Instead, I want you to take these questions seriously, wrestle with them deeply, and begin the journey of becoming a lifelong learner. There is so much to explore, and college provides a unique context for this kind of mental wrestling match. Students who enter their college years knowing the right questions are far more prepared for college than those who think they have all the answers.

Each chapter concludes with interviews with real college students, followed by questions for individual reflection and group discussion (your friends may want to join in on the fun!). The last chapter is a collection of resources that will help you make the most of your time in college. If all goes as planned, this little book will get you to ask even more questions, and the additional resources should come in handy. Oh, and before I forget: some of those *don'ts* are pretty good advice too. I'll assume that you already understand the pitfalls of too much partying. So don't get drunk or have sex. And please keep reading. You'll make my mother proud!

What Kind of Person
Do You Want
to Become?

1

Following Jesus During the Critical Years

There was snow on the ground, the sun was shining, and I was on my way back to my dorm room after class. Someone was screaming and running around a tree. As I approached, I noticed that this person wasn't wearing shoes or a shirt. He was focused and angry. Curious, and a bit scared, I asked, "What are you doing?" (Remember, this book is about learning to ask good questions. Not too shabby, huh?) If being shoeless and shirtless in the middle of winter wasn't enough evidence, the slurred speech and smell of his breath sealed the deal. He had been drinking. He whispered his answer to my question: "I'm trying to kill a squirrel. In order to kill a squirrel, you have to become a squirrel." Interesting. You learn something new every day![1]

This story has stuck with me because of how "normal" it was at the time. I had a conversation with a half-naked squirrel hunter and then grabbed dinner. A nineteen-year-old "man" was simply spending his Thursday afternoon drinking beer and trying to kill a squirrel with his bare hands. No one seemed to think that this was abnormal activity. He was being a college student, doing what college students do. The justification goes something like this: College is a time for you to have fun. Before you graduate to the "real world," make sure you have as much fun as you possibly can. Try not to cause too much damage (squirrels excluded), and don't get arrested—especially if you're an education major. Nobody hires a teacher with a record. Popular movies about campus life often reinforce these behaviors by making it almost impossible to imagine college in any other way.

> "Fat, drunk, and stupid is no way to go through life, son."
>
> Dean Vernon Wormer

Please don't misunderstand me. College can be fun. But you need to be careful. The experts tell us that the years between eighteen and twenty-five are considered the critical years—that is, the most shaping and influential. Every major decision that molds you for the rest of your life is typically made during this time. What kind of education will you seek? How seriously will you take your faith? Will you worship regularly at a local

18

church? Where will you work? Will you choose a spouse? Will you become a squirrel? Will you align yourself with a political party? What will be the central convictions of your life? How will you develop these convictions?

Did You Know? The National Study of Youth and Religion found that teenagers who establish devotional habits of praying and reading Scripture are more likely to do so as adults.

Let me put this into perspective. Take a few minutes to think about your life story. If you were to write an autobiography, the table of contents would look something like this:

Chapter 1: Birth
Chapter 2: Baby
Chapter 3: Toddler
Chapter 4: Elementary School
Chapter 5: Friends
Chapter 6: High School
Chapter 7: College (Critical Years: 18–25)
Chapter 8: ?
Chapter 9: ?
Chapter 10: ?

As you think about the most important chapters in your life story, I'm sure you would want to add some more (sports, vacations, church), but the point of the

> *"Try not to become a man of success, but rather try to become a man of value."*
>
> Albert Einstein

exercise is to get you to ask one really big question. As you get ready to enter your *most* critical years, what kind of person do you want to become? At the moment, chapters 8 through 10 are unwritten, but chapter 7 (the critical years) will give direction to the rest of your story. One expert on the "critical years" put it like this:

> What kind of person are you going to become? I'm not talking about the courses you want to take or the kind of job you want to get someday; I'm talking about the qualities you want to have. Do you desire to be wise, fair and honest—or foolish, unfair and crooked? Kind, loyal and reliable—or mean, backstabbing and unreliable? Brave, faithful and pure—or cowardly, weak and stained? Maybe you've thought about the kind of person you want to become but not about how to become that person. Every act, every decision, every thought will move you either a little closer to being that kind of person—or push you a little further away.[2]

Read the list of adjectives again: wise, fair, honest, kind, loyal, reliable, brave, faithful, and pure. My guess is that you want these adjectives to describe you. Deep down, I don't think anyone wishes to be foolish, unfair, crooked, mean, backstabbing, unreliable, cowardly, weak, and stained. But too often, if students are not intentional and careful about how they approach these critical years, the negative adjectives slowly take over.

I've seen it. Cheating on a test in chapter 7 often develops into cheating on taxes in chapter 10. Having multiple sexual partners in chapter 7 makes it really difficult to

"These are the years when a man changes into the man he's going to become for the rest of his life; just be careful who you change into."

Uncle Ben Parker

"settle down" and be faithful to a spouse in chapter 9. You may think it's easy to turn into a squirrel in chapter 7 and then turn back into a human, but before you know it you're on a steady diet of nuts and all your friends have bushy tails in chapter 8. You get the idea.

Don't just take my word for it. Spider-Man's uncle, Ben Parker, knew a thing or two about the critical years. He offered this advice to his nephew Peter (aka Spider-Man): "These are the years when a man changes into the man he is going to become for the rest of his life; just be careful who you change into." Of course, had he been talking to his niece, he would have included women as well. We all need to be careful about the

Did You Know? According to a study by the Josephson Institute of Ethics, cheaters in high school are far more likely as adults to lie to their spouses, customers, and employers, and to cheat on expense reports and insurance claims.

kind of person we become during the critical years. "Every act, every decision, every thought" is moving you in one direction or the other. Just be careful with the direction you're heading.

Student Interviews

Profile	
Name:	Christie
Interests:	reading, sports, movies, family
Favorite Music:	all kinds
Favorite TV Shows:	*So You Think You Can Dance*, *King of Queens*
Favorite Movies:	*Hitch*, *Jerry Maguire*
Favorite Books:	*The Count of Monte Cristo*
Favorite Quotations:	"People don't plan to fail, they fail to plan."

■ **Would you say that your time in college has changed you? How so?**

Yes. I gained great respect for those I encountered who were both academic and religious. I learned about Jesus and nonviolent resistance and this opened me up to what faith in action has to do with societal and personal change. Also, it was during this time that I met my husband, realized my desire to work with youth in "out of school settings," and did my own laundry for the first time.

Were you surprised by those changes?

I held some negative stereotypes of religious people and then I became a Christian in college. I remember my freshman year, a girl on my floor was engaged and I thought it was ridiculous to be engaged in college, and during my senior year I got engaged! When I went to college, I think I was interested in counseling and hadn't pinpointed what area or recognized that my psychology major had a lot more to it than just counseling.

Profile	
Name:	Erin
Interests:	learning to play band instruments, playing fetch
Favorite Music:	Contra dance music
Favorite TV Shows:	*Arrested Development, Project Runway, The Office, 30 Rock*

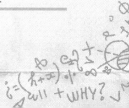

■ **Researchers say that the college years are critical to your formation as an adult. Do you agree?**

I don't think that if someone doesn't attend college after high school that they will somehow have trouble entering into adulthood. However, I do agree that the college years are formative ones. I think that for most students, college is a transitional period where you have most of the responsibilities of an adult but with a built-in community of classmates, roommates, and maybe teammates to help you navigate through your learning and living experiences. College is a time when many students challenge their way of thinking, checking to see if their beliefs are actually their beliefs or their parents' or friends' beliefs.

■ **What changes did you see in the Erin that entered college and the Erin that graduated?**

I think the Erin that entered college was very sure of what she believed but wasn't necessarily sure why or how to explain why. She was fairly certain that choosing a college was the hardest decision she would ever have to make. She knew who she was and the kind of person she wanted to become. The Erin that left college had started thinking about the "why" more. She had many meaningful conversations in classes and with friends that made her realize that people come from different places and worldviews and that dialogue is important. She was absolutely certain that the college decision was *not* her most difficult one but felt equipped to handle the world outside of college.

Going Deeper

1. When you think of college, what images come to mind? Where do the images come from? How does popular culture (e.g., movies and television) portray college life? Do you think you have a realistic picture of what college will be like? Why or why not?

2. Read Galatians 5:16–26. What is Paul's basic message about the fruit of the Spirit in this passage? How might this apply to the way you approach the critical years?

3. You don't just wake up one morning and decide to exhibit the fruit of the Spirit. Spiritual growth takes time and effort. What do you think are some spiritual disciplines that will need to be practiced during the critical years to ensure that this is the direction your life is going?

Why Are You Going to College?

2

Finding Your Place in God's Story

A few years ago I was working out at a local fitness center. It was early in the morning and only one other person was there. The radio station we were listening to announced that someone had recently won the big Powerball lottery worth $200 million. The disc jockey commented that the son of the man who won the money dropped out of college the very next day. The other person in the gym with me remarked, "If I won $200 million I wouldn't go to college either." Would you?

There is a popular poster on display in many residence halls across the country. The image is an enormous mansion with a five-car garage. It sits on top of a hill overlooking a body of water, and there are no neighbors in sight. The top of the poster reads: "Justification for higher education."

Now, I'm not sure what I'd do with $200 million (give it all to the poor?). And let's be honest, we all have a soft spot for waterfront property. But is earning more money and living in a mansion the only reason to go to college? Even the main reason? Let me ask you this: do you even know why you are going to college?

> **Did You Know?** According to the American Enterprise Institute, less than 55 percent of first-time students at four-year colleges graduate within six years, and at many colleges and universities students have a one in three chance of earning a degree.

For many students, going to college is simply the assumed next step after high school. That was certainly true for me. Since about the time I could say the word "college," I knew I was going. I never gave it a second thought. As I look back on my life, however, I wish someone would have asked me why I was going. Being forced to think about reasons for going to college would have kept me more focused and helped me to make the most of the opportunities that I was given. Early on in my college experience I didn't realize how much I was allowing our cultural story to answer this question for me. Let me explain.

A famous philosopher once said something that helped me to better understand how stories work in our world. He wrote, "I can only answer the question 'What am I to do?' if I answer the prior question 'Of what story do I find myself a part?'"[1] For our purposes, we can restate this as follows: "I can only answer the question 'Why am I going to college?' if I answer the prior question 'Of what story do I find myself a part?'" On what story is your life based? All people live their lives based on a grand, overarching story that gives meaning and shape to life. If you've grown up in a church or in a Christian family, more than likely you have been shaped by the story of the Bible. Hopefully you have come to realize that the Bible is not just a rule book telling us what to do or not to do, but is a coherent story that offers a certain perspective on life. When you go to college, you will notice very early on that not everyone lives life based on the biblical story. This probably isn't a surprise to you, but you need to know the difference it makes when it comes to education. We can't let other stories tell us what education is for.

My workout partner's remark and the "Justification for higher education" poster remind us of the world's story. It goes something like this: Life is about you. A successful life involves making a lot of money and having a lot of stuff. You are going to high school and then to college, where you will get a degree so that you can get a high-paying job, so that you can make a lot of money, so that you can retire and move to Florida. This story is often referred to as the "American Dream." People can

31

live by this story without even knowing it or being able to articulate it. It is the approved meaning-of-life story for the majority of society. Education—a smaller part within that bigger story—is seen as a ticket to moving up the social ladder.

> *"You are educated. Your certification is in your degree. You may think of it as the ticket to the good life. Let me ask you to think of an alternative. Think of it as your ticket to change the world."*
>
> Tom Brokaw

Please don't misunderstand me. I am not saying that college isn't an important stop on the road to a successful adulthood. College can and should be an important step to getting a job and making a living. I am suggesting, however, that for Christians, finding their place in the American Dream story shouldn't be the primary reason for going to college. If it is, you are allowing a story other than the Bible to shape your life.

The biblical story is about God. It's not about you. It's not about how much money you can make and buying a lot of stuff. The biblical story, the true story of the world, is about a loving God who has created you in his image. He has given you a mind to think and gifted you to serve him, all so you can glorify his name and enjoy him forever. You are to live and move and have your being in him. As you do this, you begin to discover your part in his story. What role will God have you play?

What character are you? God's story—his purposes and plans—is the story you have been called into.

Where do education and college fit within God's story? For those shaped by the biblical story, college is about:

> "A proper education enables young people to put their lives in order, which means knowing what things are more important than other things; it means putting first things first."
>
> Wendell Berry

Developing your mind. Jesus said you must "love the Lord your God with all your heart and with all your soul and with all your mind and with all your strength" (Mark 12:30). Loving God with your mind means taking academics seriously, thinking critically, and turning knowledge into wisdom. It's about being more concerned with learning and less concerned with grades. Don't tell your parents I said that.

Discovering your gifts. College presents a remarkable opportunity to think more deeply about how God has gifted you and how you could use those gifts in service to God and neighbor. The apostle Peter wrote, "Each one should use whatever gift he has received to serve others, faithfully administering God's grace in its various forms" (1 Peter 4:10). The beauty of the biblical story is that when God calls us to participate in his story, he gives us the gifts to play our roles well. Of course, this has huge implications for your choice of classes, your major, and your career goals.

Discerning God's call. Too often we think that the only people who are "called" are pastors or missionaries. The fact is that we are all called to serve God wherever he places us. Where might God be calling you now and after college? Your time in college provides a unique context for reflecting on God's call on your life. Take advantage of it. You will never have this kind of time again.

Did You Know? Many students who are not sure why they are going to college take a gap year. A gap year "is a break from formal education in order to become immersed in another culture, to volunteer domestically or abroad, to gain experience and maturity, to improve your skills in a sport, language, the arts, or academics, or take on some combination of any of these things."[2] Visit www.cpyu.org/gapyear to see a list of Christian gap year opportunities.

One theologian provides a nice summary of the place of education in God's world: "One way to love God is to know and love God's work. Learning is therefore a *spiritual* calling: properly done, it attaches us to God. In addition, the learned person has, so to speak, more to be Christian *with*."[3] Learning is a calling. If we do it well, we are attached to God and we have more to serve him with. This is the vision we need: *college is about increasing our serviceability for God.*

Here's the kicker: while the biblical story is much more adventurous and satisfying, it's not easy to live out. The "me story"—accumulating money and stuff—

can be much simpler, and many leaders at your school are prepared to help you choose it. A life based on the true story of the world, following in the footsteps of its hero, Jesus, will require sacrifice and courage. It won't be easy to go to college to develop your mind, discover your gifts, and discern God's call, but it will be worth it. Are you up for the challenge?

Student Interviews

Profile

Name:	Molly
Activities:	hiking, running, kickball, playing outside, gardening, reading, studying, games, road trips
Favorite Music:	Sugarland, Rascal Flatts, Jack Johnson, DMB, Jars of Clay, Gaelic Storm
Favorite TV Shows:	*Big Bang Theory*, *How I Met Your Mother*, *The Cosby Show*, *American Idol*, Discovery Channel
Favorite Movies:	Lord of the Rings trilogy, Disney movies, *Love Actually*, *Fiddler on the Roof*, *Sweet Home Alabama*, *Planet Earth*

Favorite Books/ Authors:	*The Red Tent, Brave New World, Little Women,* Jodi Picoult, C. S. Lewis, Mary Higgins Clark, Lauren Winner, N. T. Wright, Rob Bell, Michael Crichton, Dean Koontz
Favorite Quotations:	"Do all the good you can,/By all the means you can,/In all the ways you can,/In all the places you can,/At all the times you can,/To all the people you can,/As long as ever you can." —John Wesley

■ **Be honest . . . as you entered your first year of college, what were your reasons for going?**

For me, going to college after high school was just the next step; it's what I was supposed to do. It's what was expected of me. I'm not sure I ever considered not going to college; it was just a matter of when and where.

■ **Did your reasons for going to college change during your time in college? How so?**

My reasons for going to college definitely changed while I was at college. My whole approach to college changed the most. I began to realize the importance of my studies and their potential impact on my life, my career, and as part of my influence on the world. It wasn't just about going through the motions to get the grades. By the end of college, I began to see the overlap of all my areas of study and integrate them into something that would be a meaningful part of my God-given purpose. I began to see ways in which what I studied could actually matter and make a difference.

Profile	
Name:	Brett
Favorite TV Shows:	*The Office, 24, The Colbert Report, SportsCenter*
Favorite Movies:	*Good Will Hunting, Hoosiers, Les Misérables,* Indiana Jones movies, Lord of the Rings trilogy, *Garden State*
Favorite Books:	*To End All Wars, Season of Life, The Fabric of Faithfulness, Jayber Crow*
Favorite Quotations:	Harry: "I can't believe we drove around all day, and there's not a single job in this town. There is nothing, nada, zip!" Lloyd: "Yeah! Unless you wanna work forty hours a week." (*Dumb & Dumber*)

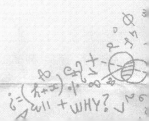

■ **Looking back, if someone had asked you, "Why are you going to college?" what would you have said?**

At first, I would have probably been startled by the question. It would have thrown me off-guard . . . isn't it obvious why everyone goes to college? But if I had to give an answer, I'd have said to play basketball and to hopefully get a degree that would get me a better, higher-paying job.

■ **Do you think your reasons were good ones?**

Well, I really wanted to play basketball in college, and there's nothing wrong with going to college to get a degree to get a job. I don't see anything necessarily wrong with those motivations. But what I realized in college was that there were many people around me who weren't really motivated to do anything. They were simply killing time before they had to enter the real world. I wanted my time in college to be different. I wanted to soak it all in and make the most of my experience. I remember a group of my friends really discussing what college was like and really wanting it to be different. We concluded that God had us in college for a reason and we needed to take it more seriously. Oh, we still had fun, but we also challenged each other to not waste our time in college and to use it as preparation for how God might want to use us in the future.

Going Deeper

1. Make a list of reasons why you think people should go to college. Are the reasons you came up with compatible with the biblical story? Which are? Which aren't?
2. If you were to put all of your thoughts, feelings, and emotions about going to college into one word, what would that one word be? Was "calling" your one word? Do you think you are being called by God to go to college? Why or why not?
3. Was college always the assumed next step after high school for you? Be honest: at this point in your life story, what are *your* reasons for going to college? Do you think it is important to have reasons for going to college?

What Do You Believe?

3

Taking Ownership
of Your Faith

Raise your hand if you believe in Jesus and the Bible."
This was one of my first classes in college, and
the philosophy professor really wanted to see a show
of hands. Well, yeah, I believe in Jesus and the Bible, so
I put my hand in the air. My hand was joined by about
twenty-five others in a class of roughly forty. I was pretty
confident with my hand waving, taking a stand for Jesus.
A hallelujah chorus was breaking out somewhere, I just
knew it. But the professor was less than pleased. In fact,
he made it his mission to see that no one left his class
believing in Jesus or the Bible or any other silly myth.
Day after day, he mounted attack after philosophical

attack against the existence of God, doing his best to reshape impressionable young minds.

The professor succeeded, kind of. He would check in from time to time, asking the uninformed "believers" to raise their hands. As the semester progressed, fewer and fewer students were willing to identify themselves as Christians. But they didn't exactly become atheists, either. Instead, most of the students simply stopped caring. Some hunted squirrels, many played hours of video games, and still others became accounting majors. *Get me as far away from philosophy as possible!* Believing in God and the Bible isn't easy in college, but believing in *anything* can be quite the challenge as well.

> *"When people stop believing in God, they don't believe in nothing—they believe in anything."*
>
> G. K. Chesterton

We are bombarded with messages telling us what to believe about the world. Television shows, advertisements, popular music, and movies constantly tell us to believe certain things. Most of the time it's subtle. Recently I had a drink that was supposed to "energize my body, enlighten my mind, and uplift my soul." I think that's asking a lot from grape juice, but it makes my point and tells us something about the culture in which we live. Do you really believe juice can do all those things? Is that even possible?

Over time, I think we lose interest. We're not sure if we can trust anything. We're not sure what truth is. Here's

44

where it gets tricky. On the one hand, we are surrounded by messages, all vying for our allegiance and trying to get us to believe certain things. *Wear this deodorant spray and you will be sure to get the night of your life.* On the other hand, our culture makes it seem like it really doesn't matter what you believe. Beliefs are "individual preferences" that can change all the time. You can believe anything you want as long as you don't hurt anyone. *Yes, you smell like insect repellant, but who am I to judge?*

> "God made man in his own image, and one of the noblest features of the divine likeness in man is his capacity to think."
>
> John Stott

Deep down, we know that beliefs really do matter. We are able to see through the lies of most advertisements, and we are bright enough to know that no one can actually disprove the existence of God. If the critical years are about anything, though, they are about honing in on the central convictions of your life. What do you *really* believe? *Why* do you believe what you believe? Have you taken ownership of your faith? These are important questions for all people, but especially for those who would raise their hands when asked if they believe in the One who said, "I am the way, the truth, and the life."

Amidst a college culture of apathy and unquestioned certainty, the challenge will be to become a true seeker. The church sometimes defines seekers as those outside of

45

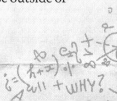

the faith, but I'm not sure that's the best definition. I think "seeker" is a good way of describing anyone who is willing to use their God-given minds in a constructive manner. One writer explains it like this: "True seekers are quite different. On meeting them you feel their seriousness, their driven restlessness. Something in life has awakened questions. . . . They have been forced to reconsider. . . . Seekers are people for whom life, or a part of life, has become a point of wonder, a question, a problem, an irritation. It happens so intensely, so persistently, that a sense of need consumes them and launches them on their quest."[1]

There will be many times when you feel this sense of awakening, when new questions arise and you are relentlessly driven to find answers. You may become frustrated because many of your classmates won't seem to care. I plead with you, don't give up! Stay on that quest! Read books. Ask more questions. Find better conversation partners. The temptation to go with the flow, to disengage intellectually, is strong. It's no wonder the apostle Paul stressed the importance of developing a Christian mind. Here's his warning: "Do not conform any longer to the pattern of this world, but be transformed by the renewing of your mind" (Romans 12:2). A renewed mind is what true seekers are after, and transformation will require some work.

Here are some key insights that I learned while in college and wish I had known before starting my quest:

Christianity is a comprehensive worldview, not just your "religion." In other words, your faith is about much more than your Sunday morning schedule. The implications of this will take a lifetime to work out, and the resources I suggest in the final chapter will help you flesh this out even more. But for now you need this term "worldview." In the previous chapter I discussed big stories and how they shape us. Worldview is another way of talking about the same thing. Here's a good definition for starters: "The term worldview may sound abstract or philosophical . . . but actually a person's worldview is intensely practical. It is simply the sum total of our beliefs about the world, the 'big picture' that directs our daily decisions and actions."[2] Your faith is not just a ticket to heaven or the "religious" part of your life. Rather, your faith should be the center of who you are, affecting the way you "see" everything.

Your worldview will be challenged. This will happen inside and outside the classroom. First, don't be intimidated by professors. Yes, they have PhDs and are very smart. But know this about faculty who are hostile or indifferent to the Christian faith: they appreciate students who care about learning, ask good questions, do their homework, and think critically. Second, the challenge to maintaining a Christian worldview is probably more difficult outside of the classroom. Here's one student's story: "When I came to college and started talking to people, I realized that I lived my life differently than the other people around me. I was challenged to think about why I lived the way I did and why I believed the things I believed. I was never in a situation where I had to do that before. It challenged me to think more deeply about every area of my life." Once again, that verse from Romans is so relevant: do not *conform*, but be *transformed* to live differently. In a culture of laziness and procrastination, be disciplined and proactive. In a world of hooking up and using others for your own gain, build lasting friendships and put others ahead of yourself. Keep in mind, challenges will come, but the Christian faith has a two-thousand-year-old track record of withstanding challenges!

> *"Faith does not deepen through being allowed to stagnate, but through being applied. In this respect, doubt is a positive thing. It is a stimulus to growth in faith. It snaps us out of complacency."*
>
> Alister McGrath

It is **okay** *to have doubts and ask questions about your faith and what you really believe to be true.* Doubting is not the opposite of faith. I have always been encouraged by the story of Jacob. God changed his name to Israel (Genesis 32), which means "he who wrestles with God." Evidently, wrestling with God is one aspect of what it means to be a believer. Read the Psalms and you will find godly people asking God some pretty tough questions. *God, where are you in the midst of this mess that I'm in?* I don't know what your church experience has been, but some church youth groups haven't challenged students to ask difficult questions about the faith.

48

This shouldn't be the case. God welcomes our doubts and questions, and they certainly don't surprise him. Some of the best moments of spiritual growth in my life came as a result of dealing honestly with my doubts and questions. But there is good, honest doubting, and not-so-good, dishonest doubting. The latter usually is an excuse for immoral behavior. Don't be surprised to come across students who say they are "questioning God" while getting drunk or sleeping around. You shouldn't use the excuse of having doubts about faith to live as you please. True seekers are different.

> "The reason many of us do not ardently believe in the gospel is that we have never given it rigorous testing, thrown our hard questions at it, faced it with our most prickly doubts."
>
> Eugene Peterson

You most likely will not come across any* new *challenges to the Christian faith. There were times in college when I would hear a challenge to the Christian faith and think, "If my youth pastor heard this, he wouldn't be a Christian either." But after a simple investigation I would always learn that the big questions people ask about God have been around for a long time. For example, many ask, "How can God be good with all of the pain and suffering in the world?"[3] That's a legitimate question that we all need to wrestle with, but it's not a *new* question. People have been asking it for thousands of years and have come out the other side firmly believing in the God of the Bible. Just know that when you hear a powerful argument against the Christian faith, chances are pretty good that you can find a thoughtful Christian response.

A life following Jesus is a process and a journey. We will never have everything figured out. Being a disciple literally means that we are "students" of Jesus. We are all lifelong learners. Like all relationships, nurturing a relationship with Jesus takes time and intentionality. Being shaped by his ways and growing in deeper dedication to his kingdom is an adventure that will last a lifetime. Thankfully, Jesus is patient with us, even when it appears we may have lost our way.

You may not be asked to raise your hand for Jesus in class, but challenges will come as you make your way through college and beyond. Some will come from professors and textbooks, others from new friends and social experiences. Nothing I can say will prepare you completely for those challenges. My hope is that you are more and more convinced of the truth of the gospel each day and that Jesus remains central to what you believe about the world. Your story, like many stories before you, will probably include chapters of deep faith and chapters of serious questions and doubts. This is the challenge of taking ownership of your faith. It won't be easy, but it's worth it.

Student Interview

Profile

Name:	Pierce
Interests:	poetry, writing, basketball
Favorite TV Shows:	*Biggest Loser, CSI*
Favorite Movies:	Lord of the Rings trilogy, *Dances with Wolves*
Favorite Books/ Authors:	the Bible, Rilke's *Book of Hours: Love Poems to God*, C. S. Lewis
Favorite Quotations:	"God won't be lived like some light morning / Whoever climbs down the shaft must give up / Earth's repletedness for the craft of mining: / Stand hunched and pry him loose in tunnels." —Rainer Maria Rilke

▨ How did your time in college challenge what you believed about the world?

I've always thought there is a right way to do things. Whether or not I was the one who knew that way made

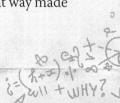

little difference. College can often appear to slap this worldview in the face. You will be confronted with so many intelligent, convicted students that issues which appeared to be crystal clear before college end up seeming very complex. College aggressively challenges your personal stances on anything from politics to alcohol, asking you to make compromises.

▓ How did you respond to those challenges?

Obviously a student will not get much from college by refusing to change on every detail of their religious views and personal opinions. This is a good thing. College made me change and open myself up, both religiously and intellectually, to ideas outside my comfort zone. However, through poor choices of my own I eventually discovered that not all compromise is good. It's very important to have a number of different-minded friends and mentors. That way you can expand your character without throwing away parts that seem "outdated" or "strange."

▓ What advice would you give new college students struggling with challenges to their faith?

My advice to students struggling with faith issues has two parts: read and talk. Reading Scripture and books on the spiritual life will quickly reveal that many students, and professors for that matter, have false and misguided views on the Christian faith. College is your path to walk; do the research that will aid your spiritual struggles. Talking both about what you understand and what you still don't quite get will help you externalize all that students usually dismiss into some dark part of themselves. You may learn that dialogue will allow you to hear parts of yourself that otherwise would keep you from spiritual growth.

Going Deeper

1. Make a list of what you think are the greatest challenges to the Christian faith. Do you have answers to these challenges? Where might you look for answers?
2. In what areas do you struggle now? What questions about your faith do you think college life will force you to ask? How can you begin to prepare for those questions and challenges?
3. Read James 1:2–5 and Romans 5:3–4. What do these passages have to say about facing trials in our lives? Why do you think it is important to keep these passages in mind when you head off to college?

Who Are You?

4

Securing Your Identity
in Christ

One of my best friends is a personal trainer. He tells me that men and women are completely different when it comes to seeing their reflections. Overweight and out of shape men often think they look pretty darn good standing in front of the mirror. *Dude, check out my six-pack. No, this one on my stomach.* Women who are toned and fit, on the other hand, will see nothing but fat and wrinkles. *If only I could lose a few pounds here—and here, and here, and here, and here. I'm sorry, were you saying something?* What's really difficult for my friend is getting both genders to be honest about their health and appearance. We all tend to see what we want to see.

Have you ever taken a look in the mirror? I'm not talking about a literal mirror. Have you ever done a self-evaluation? Have you ever asked this tough question of yourself: *Who am I?*

"An unexamined life is not worth living."

Socrates

The summer before my freshman year of college, I took a look in the mirror. I literally stared at myself for several minutes. I was eighteen, a good student, had a basketball scholarship, a beautiful girlfriend (who is now my wife!), and was either going to be an award-winning journalist for *Sports Illustrated* or a successful lawyer like the heroes of John Grisham novels. On the outside I had everything together. Then I did something that changed my life forever. I stopped in front of my bathroom mirror, took a long look, and mouthed three simple words: *Who are you?*

My answer, or lack of an answer, revealed some inner turmoil that was hard to deal with. I realized that I was wearing different "masks" for different people. I was a different person to my parents, to my girlfriend, to my coach, to my teachers. So much so, that I wasn't sure who I really was. While painful at the time, this identity crisis sent me on a journey to discover my *true* identity. It forced me to ask difficult questions of myself before it was too late—before other people began to answer them for me.

Transitioning from high school to college creates many challenges, but the challenges to your identity and self-worth may be the hardest of all. What's more, college provides an opportunity to be anonymous, to start over, to create a new identity. You can be almost anyone you want to be. Who are you, *really*? Having trouble coming up with an answer? Don't worry, our culture provides many answers to choose from, even if we don't recognize them as such. The problem, of course, is that the world's answers are not ultimately satisfying. Here are a few answers that you will be confronted with and tempted to use. The world tells us:

You are what you buy. We try to purchase an identity. College students are an ideal market, spending $200 billion each year. Think about it: thousands of eighteen- to twenty-two-year-olds, all hanging out together and discussing what's cool and what isn't, what looks good and what doesn't, what technology will solve all of their problems and what won't. Today's commercials rarely inform us of a product's merits. They're more interested in selling an experience or an identity. Next time you're watching TV, ponder what is actually being sold. This is one of the reasons why credit card debt is such a problem for college students. When you walk onto campus your first semester, don't be surprised when you are bombarded with credit card companies offering you free gifts to sign up. You will be enticed by creative gimmicks (free food, free stuff) to start an account. Be careful; with that credit card in hand, you will then be tempted to purchase all kinds of things that you don't need. Before heading to college, think through how you will manage your money.

You are how you look. Many college students wrestle with body image issues. Here's how one student described her experience:

> It's hard to feel beautiful when looking through fashion magazines. It is even harder at college. College is like walking through a fashion magazine 24/7. It's difficult enough to stay on top of schoolwork, nevertheless to stay on top of what you look like in comparison to the hundreds of other young, beautiful women walking around campus. It is the only time in life where you are surrounded by people your own age trying to look their best. It makes you question your own identity and self-worth. It's not easy.

Many students, including men, suffer from eating and exercise disorders. There is intense and unrealistic pressure to look a certain way on campus, and many students cave under that pressure. Magazine cover photos, super models, and movie stars become the standard, beckoning us from all directions: *if you look like this, you will be loved.* And we often get caught trying to measure up. It's not easy, indeed.

Did You Know? College seniors with at least one credit card graduate with an average of $4,138 in credit card debt.

You are what you do. Have you listened to your parents when they meet new people? After they get the names out of the way, the next question is usually "What do you do?" An occupation says a lot about a person in American culture. Many people think that what we do for a living determines the kind of person we are. On the surface, there doesn't appear to be anything wrong with this. We have been cre-

> **Did You Know?** On average, five thousand logos, labels, announcements, and advertisements flicker across our consciousness daily!

ated by God to *do* things for him and for others. The danger is when we begin to find our identity in what we can do or accomplish. At that point it's no longer about God, it's about us. I'll say more about this at the end of the chapter.

You are somebody if you are accepted by the "right" people. We all have our own idea of who the right people are. We often find ourselves doing things that we wouldn't normally do in order to gain the attention of the "in" crowd. The tendency to wear different

> *"This sounds very simple and maybe even trite, but very few people know that they are loved without condition or limits."*
>
> Henri Nouwen

masks for different people runs pretty deep. Maybe you wear a mask at school, doing things to fit in with a certain crowd. Perhaps you wear a mask at church, acting differently around your Christian friends. Some of you wear a mask online, filling in your MySpace or Facebook profile with information that depicts an idealized image of yourself. These temptations won't go away when you arrive on campus.

> *"I'm absolutely convinced that nothing—nothing living or dead, angelic or demonic, today or tomorrow, high or low, thinkable or unthinkable—absolutely nothing can get between us and God's love because of the way that Jesus our Master has embraced us."*
>
> Romans 8:38–39, *The Message*

Once again, we need to allow the biblical story to shape our identity. The biblical story explains that you are a child of God. Now, that can sound a bit clichéd, but I have found it to be a very enlightening and quite satisfying answer to the question "Who am I?" *Who are you? You are a child of God.* It seems simple—almost too simple—to be an adequate answer to the complex question of personal identity. And yet . . . and yet I have discovered the richness and depth of this phrase, of this answer. It's not simplistic at all.

On the journey to college, knowing you are a child of God and having your identity secure in him will make all the difference in the world. Think about it: if your identity and worth are determined by being a child of God, then you already are *somebody* even before you *do* anything. This is liberating! You don't have to continually prove yourself

62

to others or do things to justify your existence. You are a child of God, completely known and completely loved by him. Your whole identity is not wrapped up in what you buy, what you do or achieve, or what you look like, and you do not have to worry about being accepted by everyone. You are a child of God; no one and nothing can take that away from you.

Sports have always been a big part of my life, and I was blessed with the opportunity to play basketball in college. I ran into some trouble when I realized that my identity, my worth, was connected to what I was able to do on the basketball court. The problem was that when I wasn't playing well, when I had a bad game or practice, I felt like I no longer had a *self.* In my mind, I wasn't *anybody* unless I could score a lot of points or win a lot of games. Fortunately, God brought people into my life who constantly reminded me that I was a child of God. Resting in that knowledge *first* allowed me to relax and play the game for its own sake. Sure, I played hard and wanted to do well, but basketball

> *"Everybody has to live for something. Whatever that something is becomes 'Lord of your life,' whether you think of it that way or not. Jesus is the only Lord who, if you receive him, will fulfill you completely, and, if you fail him, will forgive you eternally."*
>
> Tim Keller

was no longer just about me. God determined my worth no matter what happened on the court.

For me it was basketball. What is it for you? Where do you find your identity? In your academic achievements? In your popularity? In your circle of friends? In your church youth group? Or do you find your identity in Christ alone?

This isn't easy. You will wrestle with this for your entire life, but it will be huge as you find your place on campus. I'm simply inviting you to recognize the tension that will always be there. *Who are you?* You are a child of God, and finding your identity in Christ will make all the difference in the world as you transition to college.

Student Interviews

Profile	
Name:	Lorraine
Interests:	playing guitar, reading, tennis, basketball, golf, photography, travel
Favorite Music:	Michael Bublé, Faith Hill, DMB, Sara Bareilles, Brooke Fraser, Erin McCarley
Favorite TV Shows:	*Seinfeld, Bones, Scrubs*

Favorite Movies:	*The Dark Knight, Pride and Prejudice, Casino Royale, National Treasure, How to Lose a Guy in 10 Days, 27 Dresses*
Favorite Books/ Authors:	*A Separate Peace, Much Ado About Nothing,* anything by Lauren Winner, Sarah Zacharias, or Matthew Reilly

■ **Would you say that in college you experienced challenges to your identity? What were those challenges like?**

I think that college forces you to look at who you are and who you want to be. There were times I was faced with "Do you want to be associated with this group or this one?" and had to figure out where I belonged instead of trying to fit in with a certain set of people. It can be hard to realize you are different as a Christian than most of those around you, and it did make me question why I should cling to a faith and morals that seem irrelevant to my peers.

■ **You seem to be pretty secure in your faith and with who you are as a person. How were you able to get through college with a strong identity in Christ?**

I don't think I would have come out of college with my faith intact if it hadn't been for two things. One was

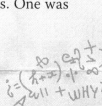

the strong foundation my parents and church had built in me growing up. Going into college, knowing why I believed what I did was paramount to making wise decisions while I was there. Secondly, finding a group of friends who believed like I did and made it a point to participate in faith-developing activities helped solidify my identity as a Christian. Knowing that I was not alone made me more confident in who I was and more able to grow in and share my faith.

Profile	
Name:	Chris
Interests:	fantasy football, backpacking, New York Yankees
Favorite Music:	ska, punk
Favorite TV Shows:	SportsCenter, The Office, NCIS, House
Favorite Movies:	The Ghost and Mr. Chicken

■ Was there a time in college when you had to ask "Who is Chris?"

I spent my freshman year at a college I didn't like while studying a field I thought I was well-suited for. After that first year, I found I didn't know what I wanted to do with my life. I no longer found joy in studying the same things I excelled at in high school. I had based too much of my current and future identity on my vocation, on what I hoped to do for my job after college. Once I realized I didn't want my identity wrapped up with what I would do for a living, it made me start to ask some serious questions.

▪ What helped you settle on an answer to that identity question?

I wasn't sure where I wanted to transfer or what I wanted to study, so I moved home and took a semester of classes at our local community college. During these several months I spent a lot of time praying and asking God to help me find answers. But I didn't just sit around waiting for God to hit me on the head with his will for my life and hand it over on a silver platter (though I wouldn't have minded it at the time!). I did my part by taking inventory of what I was good at and the gifts and abilities God had given me. I had conversations with my parents and close friends about what steps I should be taking next in my life. I believe God was ultimately using this time to shape my identity and gently nudge me in the right direction to become *who* he desired me to be, even though my future wasn't as clear as I would have liked it to be.

Going Deeper

1. Pick up a magazine and look at the advertisements. What is being sold? Are the ads really selling a product or an identity?

2. Where is your own identity most challenged now? Why is it often difficult for you to find your identity and worth in being a child of God?
3. How do you think your identity will be challenged in college?

With Whom Will You Surround Yourself?

5

Connecting with Christian Community

few years ago there was an article in the local newspaper about a woman who turned 102 years old. When asked what she thought was the best thing about being 102, she responded, "No peer pressure." That's worth considering. When you're 102, you don't have many peers!

I'm not sure what you think of peer pressure. You are probably sick of hearing that term. But whether or not we feel like peer pressure still affects us, we can't ignore the fact that all these questions of the college years—What kind of person will I become? Why am I going to college? What do I believe? Who am I?—will be worked out in the

> *"The values of the world we inhabit and the people we surround ourselves with have a profound effect on who we are."*
>
> —Malcolm Gladwell

context of other people. These people include roommates, hall-mates, teammates, friends, boy/girlfriends, mentors, professors, sororities, fraternities, clubs, and religious groups. And when you arrive at college, you'll be surrounded by people who don't know you. Your high school friends, neighbors, family, and others who have known you well may feel (or actually be) oceans away. Most likely, you'll be sharing a small amount of square footage with and sleeping one bunk away from a perfect stranger.

The campus activities fair will offer you 1,001 clubs to join. The upperclassmen will be walking around with Greek letters on their chests that let you know who *their* friends are. And the campus ministries may be as diverse as the Greek scene. Where do you start? Who will your friends be? These are important decisions that will shape the context in which you'll answer many other questions over the course of your time at college. Believe me, the people you choose to have around will have a great impact on

> *"Become wise by walking with the wise; hang out with fools and watch your life fall to pieces."*
>
> —Proverbs 13:20, *The Message*

how you live. Your beliefs affect your behavior, and your friends do too!

If you are going to be serious about going to college—not just to get a degree to get a job (the world's story), but in order to increase your serviceability for God by developing your mind, discovering your gifts, and discerning God's call (the biblical story)—you will need to surround yourself with like-minded people who share a similar vision. This is more difficult than it sounds. According to a recent study, many Christian students stop going to church after high school. Now get this: 80 percent of the "church dropouts" never intended to leave the church.[1] It wasn't planned. So how does that happen? It's because many students fail to realize that connecting to Christian community takes effort. You need to be intentional to make it happen. Here are a few things to keep in mind as you seek out Christian community:

"The best thing that anybody ever said to me is that you're only as good as the people you associate with. Look at the five friends that you spend the most time with—that's who you are."

Will Smith

Think through campus ministry choices. Typically, during the first few weeks of the semester, a college activities fair provides an opportunity for students to get involved on campus. Some colleges have multiple campus

73

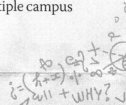

Did You Know? You can find Christian community at your college before you even get there! Here are tips for making connections before arriving on campus:

- Search the college website for "religious life." Most schools will list Christian groups on campus as well as nearby churches. If contact information is available, email or call one of the leaders.
- Ask your pastor about good churches near the college you will be attending.
- Visit www.cpyu.org/collegegroups for more tips on finding Christian community as well as a list of national Christian organizations.

ministry options. These are essentially like collegiate youth groups where students typically gather for worship, Bible study, and discussion. Here are some things to think about and ask as you approach different campus ministry groups: What kind of campus ministry do you want to be a part of? A place to ask questions? A place to study the Bible? A place where you'll find a mentor? A place that is specific to a denomination or particular Christian tradition? A place that will offer you leadership opportunities? A place that you could bring non-believing friends? Having a clear sense of the kind of group you want to be a part of can help you narrow down your decision.

Don't put off finding and committing to a campus ministry. Of course, it's never too late to find and join a Christian campus group, but it gets harder to fit it into your schedule the longer you wait. So dive right in. Check out a couple groups with the idea that you're looking for one to call home.

Go to church. It will be hard to adjust to a new worship setting, especially if you have had a good experience at home. Just remember: no church is perfect. No church will be exactly like your church at home. But it is essential that you connect to the larger body of Christ. Intergenerational community is vital. In college you are almost always around people your own age, but church services place you around older and younger people. Don't be surprised if someone invites you over for a meal—and go!

There is another reason why it is often difficult for students to get involved in Christian community while in college: the temptation to conform to the social patterns of college life is strong. Many students have a difficult time imagining that college life can be any different. But it can be. There is more to life than getting drunk every weekend. The best way to combat the pressure to conform is to find others who are trying to resist the pressure as well. Set boundaries. Know your limits. There are places that just aren't safe for you to

*"The church is first and foremost a **community**, a collection of people who belong to one another because they belong to God, the God we know in and through Jesus. Though we often use the word 'church' to denote a building, the point is that it's the building **where this community meets**."*

N. T. Wright

> *"There is no way we can follow Jesus alone. We can follow him only in community with others. Just spilling coffee on one another Sunday morning isn't community.*
>
> Tom Sine

be. Having boundaries is a way to ensure that your story doesn't have a few bad chapters.

Earlier I tried to get you to think about your life story, about the direction that your story is going to take, and about these next few critical college chapters of your story. Remember, your story is not about you. It's about finding your place in God's story. But it's also not about you in another way: there are other people in this story. There are other characters who will often determine the way your story will go. Surrounding yourself with a good cast of characters is crucial to transitioning well. The cast you choose should include people who will care for you, look out for your well-being, and bring you along in the faith. Choose wisely.[2]

Student Interviews

Profile	
Name:	Brea
Interests:	Hobbit-like things, such as eating, sleeping, running in fields, fireworks, adventures

Favorite Music:	U2, Sara Groves, Over the Rhine, Our Lady Peace, Red Hot Chili Peppers, country music
Favorite TV Shows:	*Friends*, HGTV, TLC, *The Biggest Loser*
Favorite Movies:	Lord of the Rings trilogy, *Big Fish*, *Crash*, *Saving Private Ryan*, *The Illusionist*, *Hotel Rwanda*
Favorite Books:	*The Red Tent*, *The Poisonwood Bible*, *If I Live to Be 100*
Favorite Quotations:	"I don't know what tomorrow holds, but I do know who holds tomorrow." "Love God, Love People, Nothing Else Matters."

■ **Why was it so important for you to find Christian community when you arrived on campus?**

I was a new Christian, called by God in January and then off to college in August. Being only eight months involved in Christianity, I knew that I needed to be fed . . . and fed by the truth . . . not an imitation, imposter, or "light" version of the truth . . . but the sometimes hard-to-hear, sometimes offensive, but always loving truth of the gospel. My youth leaders in high school strongly encouraged us all to get hooked into a Christian community early. They had been my spiritual leaders in my journey to Christ, so I trusted their opinion. They also checked up on me occasionally via email, which spurred me on despite the challenging environment of college.

How did you go about finding good community?

I first reached out of my comfort zone and found some awesome friends who were Christians. Really all of the "transition to college" is reaching out of your comfort zone. I remember seeing a girl with a T-shirt on that said something about a missions trip, so I asked her about it and the rest is history. She had met another Christian through soccer, and she had met another through field hockey, and the network grew. Together the five of us would go "church hopping" to find a church that taught us the gospel and "campus ministry hopping" for the same reason. I think we found good community with each other, and the vulnerability that college causes made for some honest discussion. Apart from our own little community, we searched for "food" at campus ministry groups and settled on the ones that seemed the most "real." Not the fluffy ones, but the ones that stirred you up inside and challenged you, the ones that left you crying, laughing, and confident that God is truly "with us" amidst the crazy transition to college.

Profile

Name:	Kevin
Interests:	family, playing golf and tennis, reading, playing the piano
Favorite Music:	Bruce Springsteen, John Mayer, Billy Joel, Steven Curtis Chapman
Favorite TV Shows:	*Survivor*, *SportsCenter*
Favorite Movies:	*Field of Dreams*, *Rudy*, *Remember the Titans*, Back to the Future trilogy
Favorite Books/ Authors:	the Bible, *Desiring God*, *More Than a Carpenter*, John Grisham
Favorite Quotations:	"So whether you eat or drink or whatever you do, do it all for the glory of God." —1 Corinthians 10:31

▪ Was it difficult for you to find Christian community in college?

It was. I was still going to church every Sunday morning in town but didn't feel a part of that community because I was a college student. I had no outlet to grow in my faith with other college students. I was left to my reading of the Bible and prayer to grow as a Christian.

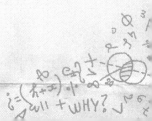

■ **What did you do to better foster Christian community on campus?**

With the help of many faithful students, I started a weekly open discussion called JCD (Jesus Christ Discussion). We bounced around from topic to topic, talking about how our faith impacts us as college students. Some nights we talked theology, other nights we discussed the practical application of our faith. There was no agenda, and only God knew where the conversation would go each evening. I know it helped me grow as a Christian. Those Wednesday nights are some of my fondest memories when I look back on my college career.

Going Deeper

1. What relationships in your life have been the most encouraging to you? Why?
2. What types of people do you surround yourself with now? Do you see yourself as someone who influences others or who is easily influenced by others?
3. Think about a time in your life where you were pressured to do something you didn't want to do or knew you shouldn't do. How did you handle that situation? Do you find yourself having a hard time standing up to temptations now? What kinds of relationships will you need to have in place in college to help you resist those temptations?

How Will You Choose a Major?

6

Putting Your Faith into Action

I recently heard a missionary to Africa tell what it was like to buy toothpaste in the United States. He stared at thirty options and eventually left the store—with no purchase. He was overwhelmed. All he wanted was clean teeth. What he got was an anxiety attack. Many of us felt like that missionary when we began college and were faced with an array of academic programs and majors.[1]

There's a small liberal arts college near my house that has about 1,800 students and offers fifty-three majors and eighty minors/concentrations. Fifty-three majors? Keep in mind: this is a small school! No wonder students are often overwhelmed and many end up switching majors several times until necessity forces the choice.

A prominent sociologist recently conducted research that explains this dilemma. He maintains that choice does, in fact, improve the quality of our lives. No question. The problem, he suggests, is that "as the number of choices keeps growing, negative aspects of having a multitude of options begin to appear. As the number of choices grows further, the negatives escalate until we become overloaded. At this point, choice no longer liberates, but debilitates."[2] It's a paradox. More choice can sometimes lead to less freedom. The amount of choices we have can be paralyzing.

> *"Education without values, as useful as it is, seems rather to make man a more clever devil."*
>
> C. S. Lewis

Of course, there are different kinds of choices. Choosing a toothpaste isn't that big a deal. Some grocery stores may even allow you to return it if you are dissatisfied. Clearly, some choices are more important than others. For instance, choosing a major. Having fifty-three majors to choose from sounds good on paper, but then you have to actually choose. You have to say no to fifty-two options. How will you make that decision? What will you decide to study for the next four years? What role will your faith play in this choice? How important is your major compared to the even bigger question of your future career and calling?

84

Deciding on a major can be difficult. I wish I had a magic formula, but unfortunately "magic formulas" wasn't one of the majors offered at the university I attended. The first thing you must consider when deciding on a major is why you are going to college in the first place. As noted earlier, most people go to college to get a degree to get a job. Deciding on a major, for them, is directly related to the kind of job they want to get when they graduate. This can put a lot of pressure on the decision. Let me ease some of that pressure.

Studies have shown that most college graduates are working in career fields that are not directly related to their program of study. I have a degree in political science and my current work has little to do with government, but I think I use my major every day (more on that later). For Christian students, while career preparation is one aspect of college, it isn't the most critical. I like the way Cornelius Plantinga describes it: "Your college education is meant to prepare you for prime citizenship in the kingdom of God. . . . Your calling is to prepare for further calling, and to do so in a Christian community that cares as much about the kind of person you are becoming as what kind of job you will eventually get, and as much about *how* you will do your job as about *which* job you do."[3]

> **Did You Know?** *USA Today* surveyed the majors of chief executive officers of Fortune 500 companies and only 15 percent of them had majored in business. A large number of them majored in liberal arts disciplines such as philosophy, art history, or literature.

85

But you need to choose. You can't remain undecided forever. College is already expensive enough! To make an informed decision, you should know the spectrum of majors offered at most colleges and universities. On one end of the spectrum are highly specialized, job-specific majors. Most of what you learn is directly related to the job you will do once you graduate, with very little wiggle room. These majors often come with certifications that need to be completed. Nursing, engineering, accounting, and even teaching fall into this category. On the other end of the spectrum are liberal arts degrees. History, English, philosophy, and political science are a few examples of the liberal arts. The major consists of a broad-based education, which, at its best, is more concerned with critical thinking skills than job-specific skills. Finally, there are majors that fall somewhere in the middle on the continuum. A business degree is a good example. While there is some job-specific knowledge acquired, there is still some room to take other courses (electives) to broaden your horizons.

Did You Know? Research by Pennsylvania State University found that up to 80 percent of students entering college admit that they're not certain what they really want to major in, even if they've initially declared a major, and 50 percent of college students change their majors at least once before graduation.

This is helpful to know before selecting a major. Here's the simple question: what kind of education do you want to have? If you are pretty sure you would like to be a nurse, don't expect too many opportunities to study literature or art history. If you enjoy studying philosophy or religion, majoring in accounting may not be a good fit. You only have so many credits (and years!) to work with, and knowing the kinds of classes you can take is an important question to ask your advisor.

I can't emphasize this enough: Christians really do need to envision college differently. It's not enough to simply go through the motions, taking tests, getting grades, and receiving degrees like everyone else. Through prayer

> *"Life is not divided into semesters. You don't get summers off and very few employers are interested in helping you find yourself."*
>
> Bill Gates

and conversation with people who know you well, you must always remain open to God's calling and leading. Picking a major may be one of the first times that you truly put your faith into action. Here are some more important questions to ask when deciding on a major:

What interests you? Spiritual growth requires discipline and sacrifice, to be sure (the Bible does speak of denying ourselves); but I don't think we need to give up or distrust our natural interests. Trust that your passions and interests were given to you by God. The writer of Ecclesiastes seems to suggest that there is something good about following your heart when you are young (see Ecclesiastes 11:9). This idea is also taught in Psalm

37:4: "Delight yourself in the LORD and he will give you the desires of your heart." Be intentional about nurturing your relationship with God, begin to see the world as he sees it, and be attentive to the Spirit as he directs your interests.

> *"God normally calls us along the line of our giftedness, but the purpose of giftedness is stewardship and service, not selfishness."*
>
> Os Guinness

Maybe you will discover that you are interested in big ideas and how they shape people and society. Philosophy or sociology would make a good major. We need Christians who are able to discern the times and know what God's people should do (1 Chronicles 12:32). Perhaps you realize that you have the gift of teaching, and nothing excites you more than helping students learn new things and grow as people. We need good teachers. The good news is that the Creator God is interested in *all* of his creation, including every field of study, and he's invited us to share his interests! Is there a possible major or future career area that God doesn't care about? Math? Geology? Physical therapy? Criminal Justice? Sports management? Computer science? Art history? Jesus loves it all, and we may serve happily in any of these arenas.

How will this major increase your serviceability for God and others? This question is much better than the typical question many students are asked: "What can you do with that major?" Let's face it, we live in a me-centered world and college is full of me-centered majors. Once again, college should be more about the kind of person you are becoming and less about the kind of skills you are gaining. Be sure to continually ask yourself whether or not this field of study is helping you to grow as a person and serve others more fully.

Who have you talked to about choosing a major? Talk with people who know you well. Ask them what they think should be your major. Talk to people who have a degree in the major you are most interested in. Ask them good questions: How did you choose that major? What were some of the most important things you learned? If you could do it over again, what would you have done differently? Community is essential to making important decisions. The more important the decision, the more people you need to be in conversation with.

> *"For the vast majority of college students, the fluid, global work environment means that what one majors in is much less important than the broader skills and perspectives that a college education will provide."*
>
> Rick Ostrander

Earlier I mentioned that I majored in political science but don't currently work in a career directly related to that field. I chose to study political science because I thought I wanted to be a journalist or a lawyer. As a freshman, I never imagined that I would be doing anything like my current vocation of helping students transition to college. But I've come to really appreciate how my major informs my work today. Critical thinking, a love of reading, and the value of civic engagement were instilled in me by studying political science. Looking back, political science was a good major for me after all.

Although the college chapter of my life story took many twists and turns, one thing remained constant: God was the author. Choosing a major is an important, sometimes stressful decision. But it isn't final. You can certainly change or refine your major along the way. Some things in life—including proper discernment about our deepest callings and vocations—unfold even as we enter the process of clarifying our call. Through it all, just remember that trusting the author of your story is more important still.

Student Interviews

Profile	
Name:	Christina
Interests:	reading, tennis, anything outdoors, spending time with my family and friends

Favorite Music:	folk, country, pop, classical
Favorite TV Shows:	*The Office, The Biggest Loser, Law & Order, 24*
Favorite Movies:	*My Best Friend's Wedding, The Proposal, Runaway Bride*
Favorite Books:	the Bible, *Twilight*

■ You changed your major after your first year in college. What motivated that change?

Once I went through my freshman year as an occupational therapy (OT) major (which had been my dream career since seventh grade!), I realized that I was a horrible science student. It crushed me to have to consider another major, but I realized the academic part of becoming an OT major might not be the right course for me.

■ How did you go about selecting your new major? Are you glad you made the switch?

I had to think about *why* I wanted to be an OT in the first place, and I realized that I wanted to work with kids with special needs. I then researched different avenues to achieve that goal, and I eventually graduated with a major in elementary and special education. Although

91

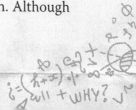

teaching was the *last* thing I wanted to do originally, once I began the schooling I found that it was a much better fit than I would have ever imagined! Now that I am an autistic support teacher in an elementary school, I realize that this is the right place for me. Also, as an added benefit, I now work very closely with an OT in the school setting. My OT background helps us to collaborate with each other, and it helps my students to have a more comprehensive teaching approach every day.

What role did your faith play when you were making these decisions?

When I finally realized that I was not going to be in the field that I had always pictured myself in, I felt a sense of loss. I also felt that I must not have listened to God like I should have, and that I must have been really off the mark to think my original career path was the right one for me. I felt lost when I realized I had to change career paths, but that sense of loss sent me to God with desperate prayers asking where I was to go from there. Looking back, it is amazing to see that God really led me into the career that is right for me, and there was a divine reason for the change after my freshman year.

Profile

Name:	Mark
Favorite Music:	Hootie and the Blowfish, Rancid, The Indigo Girls, Ricky Martin
Favorite TV Shows:	*Three's Company, Pinwheel, Sally Jesse Raphael, The Fall Guy*
Favorite Movies:	*Look Who's Talking Too, Back to School, Home Alone, The Sandlot, Big Fish*
Favorite Books:	*The Outrageous Idea of Academic Faithfulness, Ordering Your Private World, Orthodoxy, Freedom of Simplicity*
Favorite Quotations:	"Success is going from failure to failure without a loss of enthusiasm."—Churchill "Therefore, do not worry about tomorrow, for tomorrow will worry about itself. Each day has enough trouble of its own."—Jesus of Nazareth "Music with dinner is an insult both to the cook and the violinist."—Chesterton

■ **Did you manage to keep the same major throughout your time in college? Did your understanding of your major change at any time?**

Believe it or not, I actually entered college as a communications major before majoring in education. Writing always came easier to me than math or science, so it seemed like a logical choice. After a year of college, I began to realize that the field of communications can be quite competitive, especially in the career that I had in mind. It was at this point that I began to think more critically about the *why* behind my major. My shift to education had a lot to do with my desire to experience meaning and virtue in my profession.

■ **What are some of the different things you've done with your major since graduating?**

Well, I'm currently teaching high school English. However, I've found that the arena of education offers even more professional opportunities for me to pursue, especially as I discover new gifts and passions that I didn't recognize eight years ago. Out of college, I spent a year involved in urban missions, which led naturally to my first teaching job in an urban school district. I later taught in a private preparatory school and began pursuing my graduate degree in school counseling. God has been faithful to lead me one step at a time. I've learned that the idea of "calling" is not necessarily a lifelong commitment to a specific niche, although it might be for some. Calling is much more about being intentionally present where God has placed me *today*. We often ask that God would make level paths for our feet, and our human desire is to see what lies ahead, miles and miles down the path. Obviously, I've never been able to see that far ahead; in fact, God has only shown me one step (literally) at a time. Seeing God's call on my life *today* and faithfully responding to that call *today* is the only way I'll find myself at *his* destination for me, and not my own, miles down the path.

Going Deeper

1. What comes to mind when you think of "calling"? Do you agree that God cares about all of his creation and that he calls people to different kinds of work? Why or why not?
2. Have you ever been doing something and thought "This is what God created me to do"? What were you doing? What gifts were you using? How often do you do similar work?
3. What is your dream job? You know, the kind of work you would do even if you weren't paid. What major do you think will best prepare you for that job? What might keep you from going after your dream?

How Do You Want Your Life to Influence Others?

7

Leaving a Legacy

You are going to die. I can still remember chills going down my spine when I first heard someone challenge me with those words. The speaker was inviting his audience to think more deeply about the life they were leading. If thinking about your own death wasn't chilling enough, he also had all of the attendants envision their own funerals. Who would come? What would be said about you? How many lives would be touched and enhanced by your life? What kind of legacy were you leaving?

We live in a death-defying culture. We typically don't like to talk about death and dying, and people spend millions of dollars each year to stop the effects of aging. But at some point we do need to come to grips with the fact that we all are going to die. You will have a funeral.

Family and friends will view your casket, pay their respects, and then eat potato salad. It happens every day, whether we like to think about it or not.

Christian funerals are often a time when the full power of the gospel is on display. The "good news" is that followers of Jesus do not have to fear death. The Christian's eternal destiny is secure in Christ, and one day he or she will be resurrected to live in God's kingdom forever and ever. The gospel has power over death. But there is another aspect of the gospel that is highlighted at many funerals: transformational power. We are made *new* in Christ. The gospel, through the power of the Holy Spirit, transforms our lives. As we nurture our relationship with God and seek to live out the ways of Christ's kingdom in concert with others, we increasingly learn to see the world as God sees it. First, we notice that we have some work to do in our own lives: repenting of sin, seeking forgiveness, and accepting God's grace. We take up new challenges of faith and obedience. This is the lifelong process of discipleship, and many funerals offer us examples of lives that were transformed by the gospel.

Second, we realize that the gospel not only reveals to us how messed up we are, but it also sheds light on how messed up the world is. The world is not the way God intended. Things are not the way they are supposed to be. A life committed to the gospel requires more than individual change. It is also concerned with transforming the world. The best funerals that I have attended have been testimonies of how God has used people to enhance the lives of others. God transforms our lives in order to transform the communities in which he places us. The apostle Paul provides a nice summary in his letter to the church in Ephesus: "For it is by grace you have been saved, through faith—and this not from yourselves, it is the gift of God—not by works, so that no one can boast. For we are God's workmanship, created in Christ Jesus to do good works, which God prepared in advance for us to do" (Ephesians 2:8–10).

> *"To those of you who received honors, awards and distinctions, I say well done. And to the C students, I say you too may one day be president of the United States."*
>
> George W. Bush

Think about it: God is preparing you to leave a transformational legacy at college and beyond. Now, we shouldn't boast about this or think we are better than others. Paul also continually reminds God's people that they shouldn't think more highly of themselves than they ought. Remember, we are saved only by God's grace. But there is work to be done in God's world and we have the privilege of joining him in transformational activities. You have the potential to have transformational influence in four key areas in college:

Transforming friendships. Over the years I have had countless conversations with college students who have

101

been frustrated by the lack of depth of the relationships they have with other students. Many have noted that true friendships are often hard to come by. Whether it's Facebook, instant messenger, or the hookup culture, one thing is clear: college isn't always the easiest place to develop long-lasting friendships. What is needed are students who take friendship seriously, who care about others, who listen. Amidst a college culture of temporary hookups and Facebook drama, you have an opportunity to be different, to be transformational in the way you approach friendship. Be someone who cares. Make friends without having an agenda. Love others as God loves you.

Transforming the classroom. You have been through twelve years of schooling, and I'm sure you have picked up some tricks of the trade. We are all tempted to go through the motions, doing the least amount of work required to get the grade desired. For many of us, school has simply become a game. But should that be true of Christ followers? You have a unique opportunity to be a witness for Christ in the way you approach academics. Believe me, it doesn't take much! Go to class, read your textbooks, participate in discussions, write papers that are honoring to God, get together with like-minded students to wrestle with what is being learned. Ideas matter. Learning matters. Just think about how colleges would be transformed if more and more students took learning more seriously. Lead the charge!

Transforming the local community. As a college student, you have much to offer the community in which you live: energy, vision, time. My community has benefited greatly from the volunteerism of local college students. Look for opportunities to get involved in the life of the local community where your college is located. Not only will it be of great help, but it will also remind you that your time in college is not only about *you*, but is about how you can better serve your *neighbors*. Developing a good habit of helping your neighbors while you are in college will stick with you for the rest of your life.

> "The goal of the Christian life is that for more and more seconds of each day what we think and do and say is to God's glory, that every moment is worship of the true God instead of various idolatries of our making or of our culture's."
>
> Marva Dawn

Transforming the world. Changing the world is quite the undertaking. I'm always a bit skeptical when I hear that someone's plan has the potential to "change the world." But I do know this: what you learn in college has implications for the way you live in the world. And the way you live in the world will shape a particular part of the world. The question is, what will you do with the things you are learning? Will you simply *use* your education to get a degree to get

> *"Is there a way to change the world without falling into one of the many traps laid for would-be world changers? If so, it will require us to learn the one thing the language of 'changing the world' usually lacks: humility, defined not so much as bashfulness about our own abilities as awed and quiet confidence in God's ability."*
>
> Andy Crouch

a better job for *yourself*? Or will you begin to make connections between your learning and how you live, in hopes that it will bring about positive transformation in society? Business majors: can you envision creating a business that is more interested in providing a product or service that helps people, instead of one that makes you a lot of money? Future teachers: are you becoming a teacher because it gives you an opportunity to invest in the lives of the next generation, or are you more interested in having summers off? Pre-med students: do you want to be a doctor in order to improve the health of society or to improve your own prestige? Lawyers-to-be: will your work bring about social justice for the common good or be used as a ticket to the good life? Every academic major and future career has world-transforming implications, for better or worse. Followers of Christ will be more concerned with how their lives influence others than with what they get in return.

104

Remember, you are entering the critical years. Decisions you make during this time will determine the direction that your future will go. Many voices will be calling out to you to follow. Here's the voice that matters most. Listen to Jesus's call: "If you try to hang on to your life, you will lose it. But if you give up your life for my sake, you will save it" (Matthew 16:25 Message).

May the words of Jesus guide you each day, may the Holy Spirit grant you the strength and courage to follow his voice, and may God bless you and keep you in college and beyond.

Student Interview

Profile	
Name:	You
Interests:	Reading
Favorite Book/ Author:	*Make College Count: A Faithful Guide to Life and Learning;* anything by Derek Melleby
Favorite Movie:	Waiting for *Make College Count* to be made into a movie
My goals for college are:	

105

My time in college will be a success if:

I hope to have a transformational influence in college by:

Going Deeper

1. What does the gospel mean to you? Do you see it more as a private message or as something that can change society for the good?
2. Think about people in your own life who have influenced you, for better or worse. What was it about them that was influential?
3. Do you picture yourself as someone who can help bring about transformation in society during or after college? Why or why not?

Resources for the Road Ahead

This little book can only get you so far. To make the most of your time in college, you will need additional resources for the journey. The following resources have proven helpful to other students. Keep this list nearby for additional preparation before you head off to college and for assistance when new questions arise.

Books Worth Reading

Get ready—you will be required to read many books in college. The last thing you might want is to add more titles to your growing reading list! But you need to. You need books that will address the deepest questions of life, questions that you wrestle with inside and outside the classroom. The following books have done that for many college students, helping them to make sense of the connection between learning and life.

Learning for the Love of God: A Student's Guide to Academic Faithfulness, Donald Opitz and Derek Melleby (Grand Rapids: Brazos Press, 2014). My friend and I wrote this book because we have noticed that many Christian college students separate their academic life from their spiritual life—church attendance, Bible study, and prayer. Too often discipleship of the mind is overlooked if not ignored altogether. This book will help you integrate your faith and learning, to discover that in Christ himself are "all the treasures of wisdom and knowledge" (Colossians 2:3). If you liked *Make College Count*, you'll love *Learning for the Love of God*.

The Drama of Scripture: Finding Our Place in the Biblical Story, Craig C. Bartholomew and Michael W. Goheen (Grand Rapids: Baker Academic, 2004). In order to find our place in the biblical story, we have to know the biblical story well. Have you ever wondered how the different books of the Bible relate to each other? Written for college students, this book helps readers to understand the Bible as one grand story and answers many of the tough questions you might have concerning Scripture. It will also generate a passion for Bible reading and study, essential to growing in faith.

The Fabric of Faithfulness: Weaving Together Belief and Behavior, Steven Garber (Downers Grove, IL: InterVarsity Press, 2007). How do we connect what we believe about the world with how we live in the world? Are there steps that can be taken in college that lead to a life of lasting faith? In this challenging book, Steven Garber offers powerful insight into how college students can go about making sense of learning and living.

The Reason for God: Belief in an Age of Skepticism, Timothy Keller (New York: Dutton, 2008). Keller wrote this book both for the unbeliever who has questions about the faith and for the believer who is looking to be strengthened in faith. He tackles the toughest questions about God's existence, the exclusive claims of Jesus, heaven and hell, the Bible, and evil and suffering, and he does so in an honest and engaging style. You will ask or be asked questions like these at some point during your time in college, and Keller's book is a helpful guide.

Simply Christian: Why Christianity Makes Sense, by N. T. Wright (New York: HarperOne, 2006). This book provides an overview of the Christian faith that addresses the deepest questions of the human heart. It's not an easy read, but will prove valuable if you give it the time it deserves.

Taking Jesus to the Movies

College students watch a lot of movies. I'd be willing to bet that many students spend more time watching films than they spend in class! The question is, how do we watch movies? Too many students mindlessly consume movies, simply viewing them for entertainment. As Christians we should mindfully engage movies, watching them with a discerning eye to determine what they are teaching us about the world in which we live. And besides, discussing movies with friends and talking about how faith relates to ideas presented in movies makes the experience much more fun! Here are two books and a website to help you get the most out of the movies you love:

> *Eyes Wide Open: Looking for God in Popular Culture*, William Romanowski (Grand Rapids: Brazos Press, 2007)
>
> *Hollywood Worldviews: Watching Films with Wisdom and Discernment*, Brian Godawa (Downers Grove, IL: InterVarsity Press, 2009)
>
> www.ransomfellowship.org offers a fantastic collection of movie reviews from a Christian perspective.

Dead People You Should Know

It's easy to forget our history. We need to be reminded of the faithful people who have gone before us, taking stands for Christ and shaping history. I was surprised to discover in college that many of the most influential people of history were Christians. They were also

Christians who I knew very little about. Examples include: Augustine of Hippo (354–430); Thomas Aquinas (1225–1274); Martin Luther (1483–1546); Blaise Pascal (1623–1662); Abraham Kuyper (1837–1920); C. S. Lewis (1898–1963); and the list goes on and on. I highly recommend the book *131 Christians Everyone Should Know*, from the editors of *Christian History* magazine (Nashville: Broadman & Holman, 2000), as a great resource to learn more about influential Christians in history. You will be surprised how often the people in this book show up in college reading assignments! Also check out *The Church History ABCs: Augustine and Twenty-Five Other Heroes of the Faith* by Stephen J. Nichols and Ned Bustard (Wheaton: Crossway, 2010). Trust me, it's more than a children's book!

Websites You Should Visit

Internet surfing is probably already part of your daily routine. There are so many websites available, and finding the most helpful sites can be challenging. Here are some websites you will want to visit before and during college. Check them out the next time you're online.

Hearts & Minds Bookstore—www.heartsandminds books.com

After years of college ministry experience, Beth and Byron Borger opened their store as a way to help people think more deeply and "Christianly" about all areas of life. They love college students and will gladly assist you as you have questions about integrating faith and learning. This website includes bibliographies on just about any topic, including your major. Be sure to check out Byron's *Booknotes Blog* to read book reviews and learn about new releases.

Comment Magazine—www.cardus.ca/comment

Based in Canada, *Comment* is the most important magazine college students should read. Each year they publish a series on "making the most of college," offering articles on every aspect of college life. As a college student you can visit the website and receive a FREE subscription. And be sure to subscribe to their weekly email featuring new articles every Friday.

The Bible Project—www.thebibleproject.com

The Bible Project is a nonprofit animation studio that produces fully animated short-form videos to make the biblical story accessible to everyone, everywhere. The website includes videos, podcasts, and study guides that explore the Bible's unified story and overarching themes and that focus on each book's literary design and historical context.

Veritas Forum—www.veritas.org

Veritas Forums are university events that engage students and faculty in discussions about life's hardest questions and the relevance of Jesus Christ to all of life. The website provides information about Veritas events as well as recordings and videos of previous talks that were given by prominent and engaging speakers.

Jubilee Conference—www.jubileeconference.com

The Jubilee Conference is an annual gathering of college students to explore the implications of the gospel of the kingdom. Students are challenged not only to enjoy the full embrace of God's love in Christ but also to begin to envision their lives as thoughtful expressions of that love in every area of life. If you can't make the annual trip to Pittsburgh, at least visit the website. You will find all kinds of resources to help you grow as a Christian college student.

Acknowledgments

This little book requires a few big thank yous. Byron Borger, Don Opitz, and Walt Mueller were behind this project from the beginning and provided valuable feedback on the manuscript. It is an honor and a blessing to be supported by two outstanding organizations: the Coalition for Christian Outreach and the Center for Parent/Youth Understanding. Thank you to the people at Baker Publishing Group, especially Jeremy Wells, who has become a good friend. My wife Heidi gets credit for the title of this book, but she also deserves credit for just about anything I do that's worthwhile. Thank you, Heidi, for your love and encouragement.

Notes

Chapter 1 What Kind of Person Do You Want to Become?

1. No actual squirrel was injured or killed during the retelling of this story.

2. J. Budziszewski, *How to Stay Christian in College* (Colorado Springs: NavPress, 2004), 23.

Chapter 2 Why Are You Going to College?

1. Alasdair MacIntyre, *After Virtue* (Notre Dame, IN: University of Notre Dame Press, 1984), 216.

2. Kristin M. White, *The Complete Guide to the Gap Year: The Best Things to Do Between High School and College* (San Francisco: Jossey-Bass, 2009), 7.

3. Cornelius Plantinga Jr., *Engaging God's World: A Christian Vision of Faith, Learning, and Living* (Grand Rapids: Eerdmans, 2002), xi.

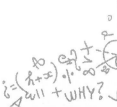

Chapter 3 What Do You Believe?

1. Os Guinness, *Long Journey Home: A Guide to Your Search for the Meaning of Life* (Colorado Springs: WaterBrook, 2001), 26.

2. Charles Colson and Nancy Pearcey, *How Now Shall We Live?* (Wheaton: Tyndale, 1999), 14.

3. This is known as the question of theodicy. Here are three books that have greatly benefitted me and helped me to wrestle the question of evil: Os Guinness, *Unspeakable: Facing Up to Evil in an Age of Genocide and Terror* (New York: HarperOne, 2005); C. S. Lewis, *A Grief Observed* (New York: HarperCollins, 1961); and N. T. Wright, *Evil and the Justice of God* (Downers Grove, IL: InterVarsity, 2006).

4. To learn more about the Fuller Youth Institute's research on college transition, visit www.fulleryouthinstitute.org.

Chapter 5 With Whom Will You Surround Yourself?

1. "LifeWay Research Uncovers Reasons 18- To 22-Year-Olds Drop Out Of Church," August 7, 2007, http://www.lifeway.com/article/?id=165951.

2. I am indebted to Susan Den Herder for her help with this chapter.

Chapter 6 How Will You Choose a Major?

1. This chapter is adapted from an article that originally appeared in the December 2007 issue of *Comment* magazine, www.cardus.ca/comment.

2. Barry Schwartz, *The Paradox of Choice: Why More Is Less* (New York: Harper Perennial, 2004), 2.

3. Cornelius Plantinga Jr., *Engaging God's World: A Christian Vision of Faith, Learning, and Living* (Grand Rapids: Eerdmans, 2002), 115.

The OneLife Institute Gap Year Program

A gap year is defined as taking a break from formal education, typically between high school and college, in order to deepen practical, professional, and personal awareness. For Christian students, taking a gap year before going to college creates a remarkable opportunity to think more deeply and intentionally about the person God is calling him or her to be. Many students who struggle in college do so because they are not able to articulate reasons or explain goals for going to college. College has become the assumed next step after high school for many, with very little thought about why. Taking a gap year forces students out of the routine of "schooling" and into a deeper relationship with God. Students who participate in gap year programs have proven to be far more prepared for the transition to college and adulthood.

OneLife is a nine-month Christian gap year program for students who want to grow in their faith, experience genuine community, serve others, and travel while earning credits for college.

For more information about the OneLife Institute, please visit

www.OneLifePath.org

Derek Melleby is the executive director of OneLife Institute, a ministry that provides students gap year programs focused on discipleship, travel, and service. Prior to joining OneLife, he was on staff with the Coalition for Christian Outreach and the Center for Parent/Youth Understanding and spoke across the country on college transition. Melleby is the coauthor of *Learning for the Love of God: A Student's Guide to Academic Faithfulness* and the author of *Make College Count: A Faithful Guide to Life and Learning*. He lives in Mount Joy, Pennsylvania, with his wife, Heidi, and three sons.

CCO

transforming college students
to transform the world

The CCO partners with colleges,
churches, and organizations to develop
men and women who live out their
Christian faith in every area of life.

Find out more at:
www.ccojubilee.org

The mission of OneLife is to launch and develop servant leaders who live out their Christian faith in every area of life.

FIND OUT MORE AT: www.OneLifePath.org

Approach Education
as Your Vocation

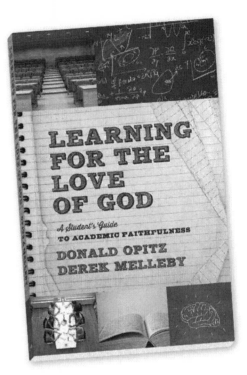

"As you get ready to plunge into college, add this book to your reading list. It will help you navigate the common landmines that can trip up your faith, and it will give you the tools you need to spring ahead."

—Kara Powell, executive director,
Fuller Youth Institute, Fuller Theological Seminary

BrazosPress
a division of Baker Publishing Group
www.BrazosPress.com